THE PARABLE OF THE COAL

MATTHEW H. SWAN

ILLUSTRATED BY MARK SWAN

PROISLE PUBLISHING

PRAISE FOR
THE PARABLE OF THE COAL

The Parable of the Coal is an inspiring tale of forgiveness, friendship and the blessings that come from overcoming grudges. This short story teaches a lesson in such a meaningful way that you will want to share it with family and friends. Matt Swan has created **one of the best fables I have read in a long time**.

—Richard Paul Evans, #1 *New York Times*
bestselling author of *The Christmas Box*

Matt Swan has provided **a timely and moving lesson on a couple of very important eternal principles.** *The Parable of The Coal* is a gentle reminder that the worth of every soul is great in the eyes of the Lord and that our lives can be forever blessed by the principle of service, not just by our service to others, but by allowing others to serve us. Well done.

—Warren B. Hardy II, Nevada State Senator

This is **a touching parable** for our day depicting a Samaritan, a brother's keeper loving his neighbor, finding the one and saving a lost offended soul. The author has beautifully illustrated the reality, opportunity, and possibility to influence for good and the blessing of joy experienced as one extends his hand in fellowship and friendship.

—Jim and Pat Neel

The Parable of the Coal brings to life springtime as it blossoms after a long winter, a change that can take place in our lives if we will but get rid of the cold thoughts of bitterness in our hearts and let in the warmth of forgiveness by helping others who may be suffering. **This parable can help you realize how important showing kindness and caring for others is in our lives.**

—Maureen Howell

The Parable of the Coal was **the best short story I've read in a long time**. In everyday life it is so easy to hold on to the negative especially when your feelings get hurt over a simple remark. We, as human beings, always seem to think if we remove ourselves from a situation, it's going to get back at others. This story puts everything into perspective—we hurt ourselves, not others, when we do this. It made me rethink my attitude toward church and people and showed how easy it can be to share our lives when we open our hearts and let go of the hurt.

—Gloria Alvey

PROISLE PUBLISHING

Acknowledgements

This book would not have been possible without John Daly who inspired me to write it.

And as always, my love and my thanks to my wife and sons for their never ceasing support.

LIFE IN SPRING

It was a beautiful, spring day as I walked from the car with my wife and son. It was just the kind of day one longs for after a long cold winter.

I noticed the various flowers planted near the building, had blossomed that very week. Their blooms were in a myriad of hues that seemed to beckon me to look at them and notice how perfect their color scheme was. Then as I stepped from the parking lot onto the sidewalk, the sweet aroma of nearby lilac bushes drifted through the air filling my nose with its heavenly, fragrant scent.

A light breeze came up rustling the new green leaves on the trees reminding me that every year they magically transform from the dead wintry skeleton shape to almost overnight bursting forth with their green cloak of leaves covering their winter bones.

Spotting a small robin in the tree, I listened to the birds chirping their melodies as if they were news commentators telling everyone that spring has once again returned to the neighborhood.

I paused a moment, taking it all in, realizing both the contrast and similarity to the circumstances that brought my family to this solemn yet personally significant occasion. My wife, Suzanne, turned with concern in her eyes, and asked, "Steve, are you okay?"

Her words broke me out of my reverie and I noticed both her and my nine-year-old son, Michael, staring at me.

"Yes, I'm fine," I said, trying to control my emotions. "A few weeks ago Edgar told me something that makes today very profound." I nodded glancing again at the flowers, trees and birds.

"Dad, what does profound mean?" my son asked.

"It means important or significant," I replied.

"So what did Edgar say that was so pro . . . prof . . ."

"Profound?" I said, finishing his sentence.

"Yeah, profound," he said, proud to master a new word.

I reflected back a few weeks ago as we spoke leaning across the fence that separated our properties. "He said, 'Life can be like the winter—cold, dark and lonely. Or it can be like the spring—warm and sunny. But what really matters is what season you choose to live your life in because nobody, and I mean nobody, can choose it for you unless you let them.' "

Suzanne nodded her head in agreement. "You know," she said thoughtfully, "based on his life and seeing him change as we did, that sounds exactly like something he would say." Then in a subdued, thoughtful whisper she added, "I'm sure going to miss him."

I noticed a lone tear sliding down my wife's cheek as she turned to wipe it away.

"I am too," said Michael in his own soft voice. "But you know what I think?"

"No, what do you think?" Suzanne asked.

"I think," he continued, knowing he now had our full attention, "I think Edgar asked God to make this day just for his funeral."

"You know, Michael, I bet you're right. Edgar would have wanted a day like today just to remind us what season to live our life in." I opened the door to the church building, letting my family enter before me as I took one lasting look at the beautiful day, feeling confident that Edgar really did have something to do with it.

As we entered the chapel, my wife and son found a seat in a pew next to some good friends. I proceeded to the front since I had been asked to speak.

I gazed around the room, noticing all the flowers and plants sent by family and friends. There were more flowers at this funeral than I had ever seen in my life.

I then began to notice all the neighbors and friends coming in to pay their last respects. I nodded in recognition to many of the people in attendance as they looked up to the front and noticed me sitting there.

Ten minutes before the funeral was to start, the chapel was full and they had to set up additional chairs just to seat all the people who had come. I looked on in amazement at all of them and began to wonder how many would have shown up to Edgar's funeral if he had died a few years earlier. Probably ten or twelve people, and that would have mostly been family. I don't think that I or my family would have even shown up.

I closed my eyes and began to reflect upon the change one person made to a whole community just by deciding to live his life as if it were springtime every day instead of winter.

As I sat with my eyes closed, I began to reminisce about the turn of events that ultimately affected our lives since moving to this rural community.

I came here to take a teaching job so I could influence others, just like a great teacher I once had who made a difference in my life. My father and mother were both teachers so I guess it was in my blood. I was also lucky that I had been very athletic, especially in basketball. I was six feet six inches tall, 220 pounds, quick for my size and had a great outside shot. I received an athletic scholarship to play basketball at a small university.

I knew I was not NBA material but at least playing basketball paid for my education and I graduated four years later with a teaching degree. Once in the classroom, I realized that my height and sheer size created an ominous presence. All I had to do was stand at my full height next to the perpetrator in class and, as they craned their neck upward, they cowered in their seat and I didn't have any more problems.

Suzanne and I met my junior year. I needed an elective and was told a ballroom dance class was easy and would also help with basketball. The first day of class, the instructor matched us up by size with our partner for the semester.

Suzanne, a dance major in her sophomore year, was the tallest woman in the class at five feet eleven inches. She had blonde hair, long legs and a slim athletic body, just as you would expect a dancer to have. She was to be my partner for the year.

The best part of Suzanne was that she was the most kind, patient, and eligible (that was the most important part to a single man) woman I had ever met. The only difference we really had was that she was a city girl and I had grown up in the country. We courted, fell in love, and were married a year later right after I graduated. I found a teaching job in the same town as the university so Suzanne could graduate. Shortly thereafter, Michael was born. I taught a few more years there but couldn't wait to get back to the country, so I began searching and took the job in this small rural farming community.

There wasn't a lot in the way of housing and we didn't have much time to look, but we felt lucky when a home with a barn, some corrals and a few acres of land became available.

I had always wanted to raise some animals and be a part-time rancher and farmer. However, Suzanne made it very clear that she didn't do animals---she was a city girl. I assured her I would take care of them and she would never have to deal with them.

Our house was next to the farm of Edgar Ekles. At the time we bought the home, no one told us about Edgar. It wasn't until a few months later that we began hearing all the rumors.

Now a few years after moving into this community, here I was waiting for a funeral to begin. I reflected how I had been influenced and affected by someone who enraged me the first time we met. Through a series of events, he became the teacher and a dear friend who had inspired me so much that it was truly a humbling experience for me, the student, to be asked to speak at his funeral.

I had visited him earlier the day he passed away and excused myself after the family arrived, knowing they wanted to have time with him alone. Later, the family showed me the instructions regarding his funeral plans he had written and given to them in the hospital right before he passed away.

He kept reminding them to have me be the final speaker at his funeral and instructed them to hand me a certain envelope and a small box located on the fireplace mantle. No one knew what was contained in the envelope or what was in the small box, but it must have been important, they said, because he made them promise him over and over again that they would get it to me before his funeral.

So there I sat with a heavy heart, holding an envelope in one hand and a small box in the other. The plain white envelope had a handwritten message on it which read, "To be opened and read at my funeral by my good and dear friend, Steve." Edgar told me he had a favorite uncle whose name was Steve, so he never called me by my last name and after that life-changing night, I always called him Edgar.

As I looked at the box, wondering what was in it, I noticed that it was finely decorated and at one time probably held jewelry. It had a note taped to it which read, "For Steve. Only you will know how to explain the significance of the contents. This has recently become my most prized possession and I want you to have it, but please share the message with others so it can change others like it has changed me." Then he signed it, "Love, Edgar."

I was about to open the box when the doors opened and I saw the funeral procession begin entering the room. My heart was full of sorrow and tears flowed down my cheeks as the coffin entered the room. I stood to show my respect and to honor a neighbor and friend who I would sorely miss. He was a recent friend, but one who had done more for me and my family in such a short time than I ever could have done for him during my whole life. Yet he always gave me a hug when he saw me and quietly whispered into my ear "Thank you, Steve, you've given me more than you will ever know."

There are moments in everyone's lives when they wish they could go back and change what they said. As I thought about the first time I met Edgar, I realized that was one of them.

THE MEETING

Someone pounded loudly on our front door. It was not a normal knock, but sounded as if a child was upset or frantically trying to get into the house before something got them. I opened the door and there stood Edgar Ekles, our next-door neighbor. The expression on his face caught me off guard as he was clearly upset.

"Keep your cows out of my pasture," he growled through gritted teeth.

In my confused state, I tried to think of something to say. "But. . . but Mr. Ekles, they get through your side of the fence. My side is fine and I fixed it before I even got the cows," I said in as soothing a tone as I could.

He stared at me. "It's not my cows getting through the fence, it's yours. You fix the fence and keep your cows off my property and I'll keep my cows off yours."

"But you don't have any cows," I said.

"Exactly my point. The fence is your problem! So fix your fence!" He then turned as if the conversation was over and shuffled off the front steps.

This complete disregard made me furious. "You fix your own fence, you old coot! It's not my responsibility! It's yours!" I knew he heard me because he just waved his hand not even looking back and continued out our front gate.

I muttered under my breath as I reentered the house.

"What's wrong with Mr. Ekles?" Suzanne asked. "He seemed upset."

"He was, but it's his side of the fence the cows keep getting through," I said, trying to justify my last comment to him. "Our side is all fixed."

"But hon, look how old he is," she said. We both looked out the big bay window to see him bent over and shuffling along the side of the road. "Look at him. He can barely walk, so how is he going to fix a fence?" she spoke with sympathy in her voice. "He probably can't even swing a hammer."

She could always see the other side of the story and be sympathetic. t was one of the things I loved about her, but I also struggled when I felt I was totally right and the other person was wrong.

"But it's the principle of the thing," I tried to argue back. "He could at least hire someone to fix it, and maybe they can fix the rest of his place while they're at it."

"I know it's frustrating," she began, her voice again full of compassion, "but you should just be a good neighbor and fix the fence. Besides, it is your cows that are getting into his pasture."

Again making the point she never did want those cows.

"Hon, it's your responsibility to take care of the cows, remember your promise to me? Now go fix the fence while I work on dinner," she said with a gloating smile.

I'm sure she was waiting for a day like this to rub it in.

"All right, all right," I said, "but it doesn't mean I have to like it. Neighborly thing to do . . . yea right, more like free labor," I muttered under my breath as I headed out to the tool shed. I teach kids all day long and have never had anyone get to me quicker than Mr. Ekles did. I continued seething as I took my frustrations out with each swing of the hammer.

"I'll (*whack*) fix (*whack*) this (*whack*) fence (*whack*) so (*whack*) well (*whack*) that he'll never come to my house again," I muttered. Giving the hammer one final swing much harder then the others.

My wife knew immediately that I was still mad and met me at the kitchen door. "Hon, you need to let it go. Otherwise it will just eat you up. Besides, I don't want to be around a grouch." She leaned up and gave me a soft kiss. "One day the tables might be turned and your neighborly act might just make a difference."

As I washed up for dinner, I remembered hearing an allegory of how we can wash the dirt from our hands but it can be much harder to wash away a grudge. I realized I needed to forget about the incident and someday apologize to Mr. Ekles for the words I had spoken. Someday, I thought, would be far in the future, as Mr. Ekles rarely spoke to anyone. I wondered what happened to make him such a grouch. Maybe someday I'd find out.

Later Comes Too Soon

Someday came sooner than I expected. As a matter of fact, it was the very next Sunday.

"We'd like to ask a special favor of you, Steve," said Henry Thompson, a church leader. "We'd like you to visit Edgar Ekles, he being your neighbor and all. He used to be a faithful churchgoer every Sunday, but something happened and we haven't seen him for years."

"Edgar Ekles?" I said in complete shock. "Just this week was the first time I've spoken with him----and it wasn't a pleasant meeting. As a matter of fact, I said some things that I shouldn't have said. He probably hates me now." I squirmed in my seat. "I'm sure there are others who would be much better at it than me."

"We've thought long and hard, and think that you, being new to the town, and his neighbor, just might make the difference," the church leader coaxed. "It sounds like you need to clear some things up with him anyway. Would you at least try before next Sunday?"

I could tell by looking in his eyes that he really didn't know what else to do. I knew I'd say yes, but wondered how I was going to be able to repent and ask for his forgiveness so soon.

"I'll try my best," I said with trepidation, "but I can't promise you I'll succeed."

"That's all we're asking," he said, relief flooding his face. "If it's to be, God will provide a way. Thank you, Steve."

We both knew this would not be an easy task, but he shook my hand with a firm confidence that made me resolve to give it a good try. "Pray for God's help and he'll show you the way," he solemnly said. "I'll pray for you, too."

"By the way," I asked, as I turned to go, "why did he quit coming to church?"

"I'd really like to know the real story. No one has ever been able to find out," he said with great sadness. "After all those years of attending every week, all of a sudden he just quit coming. That's why I'm hoping you can be the miracle in God's hands to bring him back. Thanks again, Steve. I'll be praying for you."

I nodded my head and left his room thinking, 'I'll need every prayer you offer.'

A HARD PROMISE TO KEEP

My son waited for me out in the hallway. When he saw me, his face lit up. "Finally," he said. "I'm starving. Can we go home now?"

"Yes, son," I replied "You're always starving. If you ever grow in inches based upon the amount of food you eat, you'll be a seven-foot basketball player and can take care of your mother and me for the rest of our lives."

"Oh, Dad," he said as we both laughed out loud together.

As we drove toward home, my son looked at me with those questioning eyes and asked, "By the way, Dad, are you in some kind of trouble or something?"

"No, son," I said. "They asked me to visit with our neighbor, Mr. Ekles."

"What!" my son said in shock. "Evil Edgar? You're supposed to go see Evil Edgar?"

"That's not a very nice thing to say," I chastised.

"That's what all the kids at school call him. They said I'd better not go out on Halloween. Evil Edgar snatches kids, drags them into his spooky old house and then feeds on them for the rest of the year. That's why we never see him in the store or anywhere else. Dad, please don't go into his house," he said with fear in his voice.

"But, son, I promised I would try and go over before next Sunday. Besides, that's just a story someone made up," I said, trying to ease his fear. "Do you know he used to go to church every Sunday?"

"You've got to be kidding me, Dad. He really went to Church? Not him! Please don't ask me to go with you to his house," he said waving his hands in protest.

"I'll go by myself," I assured him. "But I don't want you calling him Evil Edgar again, do you hear?"

"Yes, Dad," he said, hanging his head.

THE COAL

The week flew by. Suddenly it was Saturday and I hadn't even made an attempt to go over to Edgar's house. My wife knew about the promise I had made and reminded me on Saturday morning.

"I'll get to it. I just don't feel ready yet," I told her. In reality, I doubted I would ever feel ready.

As the afternoon crept toward evening, I knew my time had run out. I dragged myself upstairs, put on some nice clothes and grabbed a heavy jacket to keep warm against the cool fall air.

I had prayed in earnest all week long and knelt by my bed for one last prayer, pleading with God to guide me.

I put on my jacket and began the short walk over to Edgar's house. As I stood at his front gate and looked at the house, I realized what Michael and his friends were talking about. It really was a spooky sight and, if I hadn't known what it looked like during the day, I would even say it was a haunted house. There were several large old trees in his front yard and with most of the leaves gone and scattered across the ground, you would have thought it was straight from a horror movie. The dry leaves rustled and the wind made a moaning sound. The moonlight shone through the branches, casting an eerie shadow across the house and the slight breeze made shapes dance on the walls like ghosts having a free-for-all party.

Edgar's front gate was sagging and in need of some maintenance. It had a weight on the end of a wire that was hooked to the gate in order to keep it shut. I took a deep breath and opened it, stepping into the yard. I let go and the gate swung back into place, making a loud clunk and rattling my nerves even more. I looked at the house again, took a deep breath and began the long walk to the back of the house.

The grass had not been mowed in some time and the path to the house was a well-worn dirt path leading to a door on the side of the house. I rounded the side of the house and saw the dim light coming from a small window next to the back door.

I stopped again to gather my courage and told myself that all I needed to do was to go into the house. If I could even get in, sit by the fireplace to get warm, say a few pleasantries, apologize for my harsh words and then be on my way, I could then report that I had fulfilled my promise and then I'd be done.

My heart pounded hard within my chest as I knocked on the old wooden door. I heard a chair scraping across the floor and a loud agitated voice saying, "Who is it?"

My voice faltered and I weakly said, "Steve Coleman, your neighbor."

The door creaked open and a beam of light flashed in my face, momentarily blinding me. "What do you want?" he said gruffly.

"I just wanted to speak to you for a moment."

"You already fixed the fence. What do you need to talk to me for? Your cows aren't in my pasture again, are they? 'Cause if they are, I'll shoot one just to teach you a lesson."

"No, Mr. Ekles," I said, bristling at the threat. "I really came to apologize for what I said the other day."

"Apologize?" he exclaimed. "It doesn't seem like anyone around here knows how. If you really want to apologize, then come inside and do it the right way before I throw you off my porch." He pushed the screen door open, daring me to enter.

It looked as though this was the only room he used in the three-story house. A bed was in the corner and a rocking chair in front of the fireplace with a warm fire blazing. A small table sat next to the window and a single dining chair was tucked underneath. The floor was hardwood with a small rug under the rocking chair. Pictures of what appeared to be family members were hung on the wall in obvious need of dusting, even from a man's perspective. The mantle was bare except for one picture of a woman, which I assumed was his wife. She had a pleasant smile, unlike her husband. I wondered if the loss of his wife had been what made him so grumpy.

Mr. Ekles closed the door quickly, then walked over and sat in his rocking chair, looked at me and said, "Well?" not even motioning me to sit down but clearly expecting me to say something.

I was at a loss for words and didn't know where to start. Even though I had practiced what I was going to say, it all seemed to have disappeared now when I needed it the most. Then I realized I hadn't even introduced myself. "I'm Steve Coleman," I said, putting forth my hand to shake his.

"I know who you are. Cut the formalities or you can just leave," he said, waving my hand off and then staring into the fire.

"Well, Mr. Ekles," I said as I began to gain a little more confidence. He hadn't kicked me out yet. "I want to say that I'm sorry for the words I shouted at you the other day when you came over to my house. It was unkind of me and I want to ask you to forgive me. I really just would like to be a good neighbor and not have bad feelings between us."

"That's it?" he asked, still staring into the fire.

"Well, yes, I think so," I responded, not knowing how to take the last comment. Usually, someone accepts the apology and smooths things over, but it didn't appear Mr. Ekles had any inclination to do so. I was about ready to leave, not knowing what else I could do, when he slowly stood up and shuffled over, looking me in the eye. Even for a man hunched over from years of hard work, he was almost as tall as I was and his piercing eyes made me a little scared. I wondered where he kept his gun. Then he stuck out his gnarled old hand. I jumped at this action, a little on edge anyway.

"What's a-matter? Can't you shake hands?" He said with a wry smile, knowing that he had a 'gotcha' moment. Still in shock, I reached out. His grip was firm for as old as he looked.

It must have been from all those years of milking cows.

"I've lived in this town almost all my life and you have been the first man to come to me and apologize. Accepted," he stated with some finality in his voice. "Thank you for coming over. Now, do you have anything else to say?"

Boy, this guy really knew how to make you squirm. I thought I was doing good just to get the apology out. I didn't think I could do this, but I had gotten this far. "Yes, there is one more thing." Just then the fire popped and a hot red coal came sliding across the floor, stopping my train of thought.

"I thought so," sighed Mr. Ekles, and he sat back down in his rocking chair. He pointed to the dining room chair and said "Sit" as if I were a dog. I pulled the chair out and sat down, looking into the fire just like Mr. Ekles had been. Just before I could speak he said, "I suppose you also want to invite me to church." He must have noticed the look of surprise in my face. "I thought so. Well, let me save your breath. I don't need to go to church with those people. I can do it all by myself. Those people haven't done one thing for me, so I don't do anything for them. Many have tried, Steve, but they just don't understand. You've been the first one to actually apologize to me so I'll let you take a stab at it. Otherwise, I would treat you just like the last one who came. He got the boot. I may be old, but I can still kick like a mule."

I had one shot. What was I going to say? Or should I just leave now before I got the boot? I stared into the fire and said a quick silent prasyer. Heavenly Father, bless me to know what to say. The fire popped again and I noticed another red hot coal come shooting out of the fire. It slid next to the earlier coal which was now cooled and black, and then it hit me. A story I had heard many years ago as a child came into my mind as clear as if I had just heard it. I knew God had answered my prayer.

"Mr. Ekles," I said, bending over to pick up the blackened piece of coal, "this coal is like you. It's been out of the fire for some time now and is black and dead. I can pick it up and move it wherever I want it to go. But the one that just came out of the fire, I dare you to pick it up." I could see by the look on his face that there was no way he was going to try.

"But if you go to church for yourself and not for others, you're like the red coal and Satan can't touch you. So you see, I don't need you to go to church for me. You need to go to church for you." I then threw the black coal back into the fire, and within a few moments it was burning bright red. My heart melted as I glanced over at him and noticed a lone tear sliding down his cheek.

"Mr. Ekles," I said, knowing he had been touched too.

"Please call me Edgar," he softly said. "And I'll call you Steve, like my favorite uncle. He was sure a good man," he said as I saw him drifting down memory lane.

"Edgar," I said as I interrupted his thoughts, "Will you let me pick you up for church tomorrow?" I waited for his reaction, I silently prayed. The rest is in your hands God; I've done my part, now it's up to you to touch him. Time passed slowly as I sat waiting for an answer. The Spirit was warmer than the fire that burned in the fireplace that night.

Then softly he spoke and gave me his reply, still staring at the coal in the fire.

Little did I know a miracle had taken place that evening. I only know that God answers prayers and I was truly an instrument in His hands. The Spirit warmed me all the way home as I realized I was going to pick up Edgar tomorrow and take him with us to church. I knew it was the Spirit that had told me what to say.

I was in awe as I watched the gruffness melt away from a grizzly old bear to a soft-spoken, broken-hearted man with tears sliding down his cheeks as he whispered to me to pick him up.

I beamed as I walked into my house. Suzanne looked up from the couch and could see the sheer joy on my face. She quickly rose and asked, "What happened? I've never seen you look this way before."

I grabbed her in my arms and hugged her tightly, hoping that she could feel the warmth from the Spirit that abounded in my frame. "He's coming to church with us tomorrow!" I exclaimed. "He's coming to church with us!"

The shocked look on her face was just what I expected and the biggest grin crossed my face.

"I would have never thought it possible," she said. "He just doesn't seem like the church-going type."

"Sit down and I'll tell you how it happened." I said, bubbling with excitement. "It was a miracle, I tell you. Simply a miracle. I know it and he knew it and now he wants to go to church.

I then related everything that had happened, and how Edgar's countenance changed right before my eyes.

"Only God could have done it," I told her.

"It was truly a miracle," she said as she snuggled into my arms.

MENDING OF FENCES

I couldn't remember the last time I felt so excited to go to church, but I was also nervous. How would the people respond to Edgar? Would they welcome him or shun him?

I called Henry Thompson to tell him what happened so everyone could be mindful of Edgar.

As we went to the car and backed out of the driveway, I said a quick prayer. Please let Edgar be ready. As I drove the few hundred feet to the old rickety gate, my fears turned to elation as I saw a clean-shaven man in a suit standing behind the gate. This was the first time I had seen Edgar in anything but a flannel shirt and bib overalls. He waved as I drove up and came out to the car. He opened the back door and slid in beside my son, Michael.

"You must be Michael," he stated. "Your father told me all about you last night. I hope we can be friends. You call me Uncle Edgar and we'll get along just fine."

Michael stared at him, not knowing what to say until Edgar smiled a big smile at him. "Uncle Edgar," Michael said half to himself and half to the man seated by him. "Uncle Edgar would be cool," he repeated.

"Hi, Edgar," I said from the front seat, "I'd like you to meet my wife, Suzanne."

"How do you do, Suzanne?" he beamed "You're every bit as beautiful as your husband said you were. Thank you for letting me ride with you today."

"You're sure welcome," Suzanne said, blushing and giving me the eye. "Any time you need a ride, you're welcome."

We arrived at church and made our way into the chapel. I was so pleased. Several people came up and welcomed Edgar to church. Many told him they had missed him and hoped they would see him next week.

The words spoken during church were very touching and, with occasional glances in Edgar's direction, I could see he felt the Spirit bear witness to him that he was in the right place.

My wife invited him over for Sunday dinner and we had a marvelous time getting to know our neighbor and new-found friend. Michael even gave Uncle Edgar a hug before he left to go. Pretty amazing for a young boy who had been uncertain about Edgar, but he had touched my son already that day. I was proud of my son for how quickly he had changed his feelings.

"You have a wonderful family," Edgar said to me as we stood on the front porch of our house. "Don't waste your life in bitterness as I have. Life is precious and too soon it's over. I let a little thing get to me and I was going to hurt them by not going to church. I now realize the only person who got hurt was me. Thank you for having the courage to come over to my house and apologize."

"Well, I think the thanks really goes to God," I said.

"Yes, last night I thanked Him for the first time in a long time, but again, thank you and tell your wife thanks for dinner. I'll see you next week. You can count on it." He stuck out his hand and as I took his, he reached around me with his other arm and gave me a big hug.

"Thank you, again," he whispered into my ear, then turned around and headed down the steps.

I watched as he walked down the sidewalk and over to his house. He was right. Life was too short to be caught up in petty things. What if I had not gone over to his house last night? I would still be upset about the fence. Suzanne snuck up behind me and put her arms around my waist. "Now aren't you glad you fixed the fence and stopped being a grouch?" she said in that I-told-you-so tone of voice.

"Yes," I said, turning around and looking into her deep blue eyes. "Once again you were right." I picked her up in a bear hug, gave her a kiss and quietly whispered into her ear, "I love you. Thanks for all you do."

"Why, thank you!" she said, obviously wondering what had come over me. We kissed again and I released her from the hug and walked into the house arm in arm.

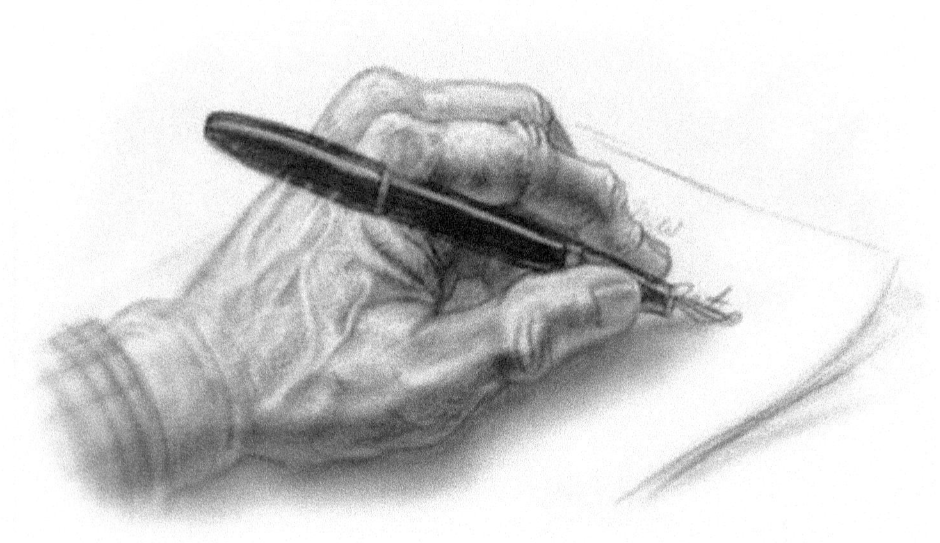

Blossoming

A few months went by and we noticed a change every time we saw Edgar. Michael now went out of his way to shout out and swing his hand in a big wave, yelling, "Hi, Uncle Edgar." Edgar would wave back and shout back, "Hi, Michael. Come see me. I have something for you!"

Michael always came back with a bag full of homemade salted peanuts. If the truth were told, I probably ate most of them. Michael also brought home story after amazing story, like history coming to life. One day Michael said, "Dad, did you know Uncle Edgar was a poet?"

"Uh no, son, I didn't."

"Well, you know how our teacher wanted us to find our favorite poem and read it to the class?"

"Yes. Did you find a poem you liked from the book I gave you?"

"Not really, but when Uncle Edgar asked how school was going, I told him about it. He went to a shelf in his room and pulled down a whole book of poems he wrote. He told me I could look at it and if I liked one, I could take it to school and read it to the class. He even said if I wanted, he would help teach me how to read it. He has some cool poems and it was hard to pick, but I finally chose one."

"You know, Michael, Edgar surprises me more and more as we get to know him. Just last week I learned that he plays the piano and has a beautiful singing voice. Who knows what we'll learn next week, but I'm sure it will be something," I said.

Turn of Events

It's funny, just when life seems to be going great, something drastic happens and sure enough I was driving one winter day and hit some black ice. The car spun out and smashed into a concrete barrier. After reviewing the x-rays, the doctor said, I had broken my left leg and would be bedridden for at least two weeks before I could get up and around, and then it would be several weeks on crutches.

I'd banked enough sick leave from my job to cover it, but how would my wife manage all the farm chores that needed to be done? Especially the cows? She tried to assure me we would get by and she could handle it. Some women from the Church had already said they would bring in food and help with Michael. I could barely move, and the doctor said I could not be alone until we saw how I reacted to the medication.

In addition to the beef cows, a few months ago we acquired a milk cow, some chickens, and some pigs. I enjoyed playing farmer and so I had, little by little, accumulated a mishmash of animals, all for our benefit, I reasoned at the time. Now I was greatly concerned how Suzanne would do the milking, feed the cows by lifting the hay bales, gather eggs and slop the pigs with the heavy buckets of feed, let alone the worst chore—taking care of me over the next several weeks. I knew it would not be easy, but she was one determined lady and I loved her for it.

My wife and I were not ones to ask for help and felt like it was just something we needed to buckle down and do ourselves. She assured me that if she needed to ask for help, she would let me know.

After coming home from the hospital and getting me set up, evening was already upon us. I could tell Suzanne was worn out, but she changed her clothes to go to the barn. A few minutes later she came into the room. With a shocked look in her eyes she said, "Who did you call to do the chores?"

"No one," I replied. "I didn't have time and, besides, I can't even reach the phone."

"Well, if you didn't, there must be an angel looking over us."

"What do you mean?" I asked.

"When I got to the back porch, I almost tripped over the milk bucket full of fresh milk and there beside the bucket was a crate full of eggs. I went and checked the milk cow; she'd been milked and fed. The cows had fresh hay, the pigs were fed and the chickens had empty nests. Some angel has blessed us this evening."

We prayed, thanking God for our safety and for the person who helped with the chores that night. That evening we realized how truly blessed we were.

The next morning, after a painful and sleepless night for both of us, Suzanne once more came in to tell me that the angel had struck again and that everything was done.

Because of the trees in our backyard we were not able to see who our angel was, but every morning and every night the milk and eggs magically appeared before Suzanne could break away to see who our mystery angel was.

MYSTERY ANGEL

Then one morning two inches of snow fell. As Suzanne went out the door, again finding the milk and eggs at the back door, she noticed some footprints.

Some time later she came running into where I lay. I could tell she had been crying.

"What's wrong?" I asked.

"I know who our angel is," she blurted out. "It's Edgar."

"Edgar!" I exclaimed "But he's eighty-years-old! How can he physically do all that?"

"I followed the footsteps in the snow right to his house and had a long talk with him." She said sitting on the side of the bed. "Steve, he made me promise to let him keep doing the chores because he felt this was some small way to make up to God for the time he missed. Here is a man who not only believes in the second great commandment of love your neighbor as yourself, he lives it. We have so much more to learn from that man."

I promised myself that I'd try to make it up to him. Yet it seemed the harder we tried, the more we realized we got behind. He was always doing something not only for us, but for others who frequently talked about an angel in their midst who performed small miracles in their lives.

After a few weeks of lying around, I told Suzanne, I was going over to Edgar's to personally thank him. "You be careful," she scolded me. "You know the doctor told you to take it easy."

"I know, I know," I said. "I'll be careful, but I just have to get out of the house, and you know the doctor said I need to start exercising; besides the snow is all melted."

"Well, I'll be watching you through the window and if you falter in the slightest way, I'm coming to get you," she said with that I'm-warning-you-now look.

I hobbled out the door with crutches in hand and stood at the top of the steps leading down from our porch. It took me almost five minutes to learn how to navigate them with crutches. I just about decided to turn around, but looking back at the steps leading up to our porch, and thinking how much effort it was to go down them, I decided it might be easier to go over to Edgar's and then call Suzanne when I was ready to leave. It was much easier to move across the flat ground and it felt good to be out in the fresh air. It was still chilly, but soon I had warmed up from the effort it took to get to Edgar's house. I knocked on his door and soon it opened up with a surprised Edgar looking out.

"Steve!" Edgar exclaimed "You shouldn't be hobbling around out here. You can't afford to get hurt again."

"You're just like Suzanne," I said. "I just couldn't stand being cooped up in the house all day. I had to get out."

"I know what you mean," he said winking. "My wife was just the same way. Sometimes I snuck out just to get away. But hurry, come in and take a rest."

Edgar pulled out his dining chair and helped me sit down, then scurried off to a back room bringing a small stool and pillow. "For your leg to rest on," he said as he gently lifted up my leg and set it on the stool. "How's that?"

"Much better," I replied and breathed a heavy sigh of relief.

"I think I'll call Suzanne when I'm ready to go."

"No, I'll call her," Edgar said. "You'll sit right here until we can both help you make it home." Then he sat in the old familiar rocking chair and we looked into the fire that burned in the fireplace. Over time, it seemed we both enjoyed sitting by the fire and basking in the warmth and reflecting on that glorious night.

"Edgar," I broke the silence, "I just wanted to thank you personally for all the help you have given our family, especially the past few weeks with all the chores and animals and everything. I am forever in your debt. You have been a wonderful neighbor and a great friend."

I said choking up on the last word. I paused a moment to regain my composure.

"Steve," he said, "it's really me who is forever in your debt. You see, several years ago, shortly after my wife passed away, someone at church said something that offended me. I vowed then and there that if that's what church-going people thought, then I would never go back to church again. I felt that I was strong enough to do it myself. I didn't need them or church. I was going to make that person pay for their comments. I decided I would hurt them by not going to church so they would suffer just like I was."

I just sat back and said nothing feeling that Edgar was once again teaching me a lesson.

"Now I know, Steve," he continued, "it really only affected me. That person who offended me, well, they kept going to church and now I realize they didn't even know what they had done. All those years of keeping that grudge, began to weigh on me and affect my attitude. Which then began to affect my health and I began to stoop over and shuffle my feet when I walked, wanting people to feel sorry for me and apologize for the things that were said. I withdrew within myself and became an angry and bitter man."

He paused as he stared into the glow of the fire. "Then you actually came and apologized to me. All those years of hatred had built a wall around me but it began to melt that night. I hadn't prayed in years, but that night I got down on my knees and thanked God for sending you. I told God that I had many years to try and make up for and asked him to give me strength to do it. Steve," he said as he turned to look at me, "when I heard you had been hurt in that accident, I felt strength coming into this old body as I knelt in prayer to ask God to protect you. I knew then that God gave me the strength I needed to be able to do those chores for you and your family. Every time I picked up a bucket or bail of hay it felt as if angels were by my side helping me to lift those buckets. It was something that I wanted to do just to feel those angels strengthen me and for that reason alone, I am grateful to God and to you for helping me change my life." Just then the fire popped and a coal came shooting across the floor. We both looked at each other knowing that this was another special moment that we had shared together.

"Edgar," I said, once again breaking the silence, "it seems we both need each other just as much as God needs us, too, and for that I am eternally grateful." He just nodded his head, then bent over and scooped up the coal and threw it back into the fire.

Once again we both watched a black coal turn bright red.

"Steve, I want you to teach others that holding a grudge can only do harm to themselves. I have paid the price for being full of hate and am now trying to make up for lost time. I hope God preserves me long enough to make amends in his sight so I might see Him once again and know that I have done my part to receive His forgiveness. Promise me, will you, Steve that you will teach others?"

"I promise, Edgar," I said as we looked at each other and bonded even more that day.

Over the next few months, I spent more and more time with Edgar, learning much from his wisdom, learning about his family, how his wife had passed away, and how much he missed her. I read some of his poems, heard him play the piano and sing. He was a part of our family.

One day, my wife called me as school was ending to tell me the ambulance had just taken Edgar away. I jumped into my car and drove to the hospital to find Edgar in a bed with tubes attached. As I neared his bedside, he looked over and saw me. A big smile crossed his face and he said, "I knew you would come. It's just like you to watch out for me. How will I ever be able to repay you, Steve?"

"Oh, Edgar, we already talked about it. It's me who needs to repay you. You have been the most wonderful blessing in my family's life," I said as tears freely flowed down my face.

"My heart is wearing out physically." He spoke with much effort. "But it's full of love and I know that when I meet my Maker, He will welcome me with open arms, due to a change in my life because of you and a piece of coal."

A Gift Most Precious

"We will now hear from our concluding speaker, Steve Coleman,"
said the man conducting the funeral. Hearing my name brought me
out of my thoughts. I arose and walked to the pulpit.

"Edgar wanted me to be the concluding speaker so I could read this
letter to you." I gently slid a finger under the flap, opening it for the
first time. He had shared many a poem he had written but never this
one, and now I knew why. He had put our experience to verse, using
my voice to tell the story.

The Parable of the Coal

One night while trying to fulfill my role,
 I stopped to visit a less active soul.
We'd sit by the fire to warm and to chat,
Then I'd be on my way and that would be that.
Then the Spirit bore witness for me to attest,
That coming to church would be for his best.
Then upon my face he did quizzically gaze
And asked me this question as if in a daze.
"Why should I go to church?" he stubbornly asked.
"When it seems to be such a burdensome task?
I can do it alone; I don't need all of you.
Tell me why I should go, Can you please tell me true?"
He caught me off guard. How should I reply?
I silently prayed to God up on high.
I pondered and gazed at the warm firelight,
Then saw a coal burning, 'twas red hot and bright.
 Yet another had fallen which had been a bright red,
 But was now cold and dark and really quite dead.

47

And in that instant, I knew God was there,
For He had silently answered my prayer.
"That coal on the floor, would you hand it to me?"
And he picked it up quite easily.
I took it from him and I tossed it around,
Then gently I placed it back where it was found.
"Now that one in the fire, would you hand it to me?"
He said, "What kind of fool do you take me to be!"
It would burn my hand and make a sore hole.
What does going to church have to do with this coal?"
 I said in reply, "You will learn very quick.
You see this is Satan's cute little trick.
If you go to church, you're like the hot coal.
It's tougher for Satan to garner you soul.
"Cause when you attend, Christ's light is there, too;
His guardian angels can now protect you.
And Satan can't touch you for he will get burned
Like the coal in the fire that you just spurned.
But when you don't go, you are like the black coal
Where Satan can easily lay claim to your soul.
For he can now move you anywhere to and fro
And silently drag you where he wants to go.
So, you see, we need church more than we'll ever know.
By going there often we'll keep up our glow."
Then I put the black coal in the fire that night
And we both watched it turn to a brilliant red light.
I pled as I left that inspiring sight,
"May I please pick you up? Would it be alright?"
A tear crossed his cheek as he stared at the coal.
"I'll be ready," he said, "I must now save my soul."

I concluded my remarks, sat down and realized I had not yet opened the box. I untied the ribbon and pulled off the top. Inside was a folded piece of paper and, lying on some cotton, was a piece of coal.

Steve,

If you are reading this, then you know I have passed on. I am now in my Savior's arms. That piece of coal in the box, well, that's the miracle coal. I pulled it out of the fire after you left and when it cooled down, I put it in this box and set it upon the mantle of the fireplace where I would see it every night before I went to bed. Many times I would stare into the fire at the red hot coals and thank God for sending you. Keeping a grudge and feelings of hate affected me mentally, spiritually and physically and was a heavy weight that I needlessly carried for many years. Your parable of the coal lifted that weight and made me realize what I had done. I have no one to blame but myself because I chose to let it get to me. That analogy of the coal changed my life and allowed me to live in the spring time.

It's now in your charge. Please continue to tell the story of the coal so that it just might save another soul.

Eternal love,

Edgar

The Inspiration and the Message

Many people have asked what inspired me to write this book. It all started when my oldest son, who was about twenty-one at the time, related something that happened to him. One day he was at the home of some friends and began talking to the father of the house. During their conversation, the father commented about life and the difficulties he had dealt with throughout most of it. It became clear that this was an angry man. My son, in an effort to try and help, related to him how life is like a coal, and how a person could choose to be like the black coal and do nothing or they could be the red coal and make their life useful.

It was several months later before my son saw his friend's family again. Unbeknownst to him, this man had embraced the story of the coal completely and changed his life. Upon seeing this family at a large gathering, my son walked right past him, not even recognizing him due to the change. The last time my son had seen him, he was in a dirty T-shirt, had an unkempt beard, and was a rough-looking character. Now he was in an ironed shirt, clean-shaven and had a glow in his face. Not only had it changed him on the inside, it had also changed him on the outside.

This touched my heart when I heard it and the impression came to my mind that this would make a great inspirational poem. Later that day, in about two hours, I wrote the poem which I called The Parable of the Coal.

A few months later, I shared this poem with John Daly, the Host of Real TV, and asked him what he thought. He told me to write a story around the poem which would get the message out better. Thus began the journey of writing *The Parable of the Coal.*

Many people have since asked about the message I am trying to convey and if I am trying to get people to go to church. The real message is that being offended and holding a grudge can happen to anyone anywhere. I just used the setting of Edgar being offended at church to tell the story and make it work with the poem. The story could have just as easily been told as if one had been offended by a spouse, friend, co-worker, boss, neighbor or someone who doesn't even know you. What matters is what you choose to do with it. You can let it drag you down, or you can get over it and move on with your life. The choice is really up to you not the one who offended you.

The other message is that of Steve, which signifies reaching out in friendship even if it might be uncomfortable. There are times when going out of your way to befriend someone provides a bigger payback then what you gave up. Imagine if Steve had not gone over that night. Not only would he and his family have lost something very special, but the whole community would have lost out. How many lives can all of us affect by just being a friend? More than we can count.

So give this book to those you feel need it or to your friends as a Thank You for making a difference in your life. It has made a difference for me, and if we do it one friend at a time, how much better we all will be.

ABOUT THE AUTHOR

Matthew H. Swan is a partner in Swan & Gardiner, LLC a Certified Public Accounting firm in Las Vegas, Nevada. He enjoys speaking and has been a featured speaker in many tax and business seminars. He grew up in a small rural farming community, played basketball and ran track in high school and at local junior colleges. Matt graduated in 1984 with a Bachelor of Science in Accounting. His first job in accounting was in Midland, Texas. Two years later, he moved his family to Las Vegas, Nevada where he and his wife, Brenda, have four wonderful sons. He enjoys music, singing, poetry, writing and just being with his family.

ABOUT THE ILLUSTRATOR

With twenty-seven years of experience in the field of animation, Mark Swan has assisted in the creation of numerous successful animation products. Mark has worked on projects for Disney Studios, Universal Studios, Warner Brothers, MGM, and on various independent projects. Mark began in television animation and, after three years, moved into theatrical features working on *Space Jam, A Goofy Movie, An American Tail, Land Before Time, All Dogs Go to Heaven, Thumbelina, A Troll in Central Park,* and *Curious George.* Because of his work on the *Land Before Time feature,* Mark was asked to help launch the highly successful Direct-to-Video sequels of *Land Before Time 2, 3, and 4,* contributing in story development, storyboards, and character design. He most recently turned his attention to illustrating books recently completing projects for Grand Canyon and Zion National Parkstional Parks.